COLORING
DEVOTIONAL

A
LITTLE
GOD
TIME

BroadS...
PUBLIS...

BroadStreet Publishing Group LLC
Racine, Wisconsin, USA
Broadstreetpublishing.com

A LITTLE GOD TIME

© 2016 by BroadStreet Publishing

ISBN 978-1-4245-4984-9

Devotional entries composed by Shannon Lindsay and Michelle Winger.

Design by Chris Garborg | garborgdesign.com
Compiled and edited by Michelle Winger | literallyprecise.com

Printed in the United States.

16 17 18 19 20 21 22   7 6 5 4 3 2 1

INTRODUCTION

Life is full of demands. Appointments, deadlines, obligations, and constant digital chatter occupy every moment and build a mountain of unhealthy stress and tension. Research shows that coloring can be an effective stress reducer, but true rest and peace are found in God. This coloring devotional incorporates these two ideas in one beautiful book.

Spend time reflecting on the truth of God's Word and be filled with the joy and peace found in his presence. Express your creativity freely as you fill the intricate images with the beauty of color.

THE FATHER'S LOVE

"If a man has a hundred sheep but one of the sheep gets lost, he will leave the other ninety-nine on the hill and go to look for the lost sheep. I tell you the truth, if he finds it he is happier about that one sheep than about the ninety-nine that were never lost."

MATTHEW 18:12-13 NCV

Regardless of how beautifully or how imperfectly your earthly father showed his love, your heavenly Father's love is utterly boundless. Rest in that thought a moment. There is nothing you can do to change how he feels about you. *Nothing.*

We spend so much time trying to make ourselves more lovable, from beauty regimens to gourmet baking, to being there for pretty much everyone. It's easy to forget we are already perfectly loved.

Our Father loves us more than we can imagine. And he would do anything for us. *Anything.*

Who do you love most fiercely, most protectively, most desperately here on earth? What would you do for them? Know that it's a mere fraction, nearly immeasurable, of what God would do for you.

**Father, I thank you for loving
me just as I am. Your love is
extravagant and doesn't change
depending on how I act, think,
or feel. You are a perfect Father,
and I love you.**

My God
is changeless
in his love
for me,
and he will
come and
help me.

Psalm 59:10 TLB

FOLLOW THE ARROW

Your ears shall hear a word
behind you, saying,
"This is the way, walk in it,"
Whenever you turn to the right hand
or whenever you turn to the left."
ISAIAH 30:21 NKJV

Decisions, decisions. It seems a week never goes by without our needing to make at least one important choice.

Whether job related, relationship motivated, or something as seemingly innocent as how to spend a free Friday, wouldn't it be nice to have an arrow pointing us in the right direction—especially if we are in danger of making a wrong turn?

According to the Word, we have exactly that. When we truly desire to walk the path God sets us on, and when we earnestly seek his voice, he promises to lead us in the right direction. His ever-present Spirit is right there, ready to put us back on the path each time we wander off.

Consider the decisions before you right now. To whom are you turning for guidance? Lay your options before God, and then listen for his voice.

God, there are so many decisions that I make each day. Some don't seem to matter and others could be life-changing. Help me to come to you first for guidance in all areas of my life. You care about each detail and you can show me which way to turn.

YOU ARE PERFECT

By a single offering he has perfected for
all time those who are being sanctified.

HEBREWS 10:14 ESV

You are perfect. Stop, go back, and read that again. You are perfect. Looking in the mirror, or thinking back over your day, it is easy to forget or disbelieve those words. Don't let that happen.

A wrinkle here, a bulge there, an unkind word, or a jealous thought cannot change the way the Father sees you. And it's how he wants you to see yourself.

The dictionary uses 258 words to explain what it means to be perfect, but we only need to know this: we are *complete.* When he chose to die on the cross for our sins, Jesus took away every flaw from those of us who love him. He finished what we never could; he made us perfect.

Stand before a mirror and ask God to show you what he sees when he looks at you. See past the flaws, past any hurt or anger in your eyes, past any perceived imperfection. See yourself complete, just as you were meant to be. See yourself perfect. How does this change the way you feel about yourself?

Lord, when I reflect on my
imperfections, it can be
overwhelming and depressing.
Thank you that you see me for who
I really am, and who I am meant
to be. You have made me perfect
through your sacrifice and I choose
to walk in that today.

You make known to me the path of life; you will fill me with joy in your presence, with eternal pleasures at your right hand.

Psalm 16:11 NIV

CHERISHED

I am convinced that neither death nor life, neither angels nor demons, neither the present nor the future, nor any powers, neither height nor depth, nor anything else in all creation, will be able to separate us from the love of God that is in Christ Jesus our Lord.

ROMANS 8:38-39 NIV

It's good to be loved, isn't it? What feeling really compares to knowing someone has run through the rain, cancelled an international flight, driven all night—for you? Even if we've never experienced it, we've imagined it in our hearts. Or else we've had the realization that we, too, would move heaven and earth for the one we love the most.

Whether husband, child, parent, sibling, or dear friend, to love and be loved deeply just may be the best feeling there is.

How much love you have given or received is a mere sampling of the way Jesus feels about you. You are cherished, loved beyond reason or measure. The one who really *can* move heaven and earth would do so in a heartbeat—for you.

Let the incredible words above wash over you as you realize there is nothing—absolutely nothing—Jesus wouldn't do for you. Can you feel his love toward you today?

> God, I feel your love today. You sacrificed everything to show me that you cherish me. You want to spend time with me. You delight in me. I bask in your love today and choose to let it fill me so I am overflowing with love for you and others.

TROUBLED HEART

"Peace I leave with you; my peace I give you. I do not give to you as the world gives. Do not let your hearts be troubled and do not be afraid."

JOHN 14:27 NIV

I can't get a moment's peace. Sound familiar? We all go through seasons where it seems every corner hides a new challenge to our serenity, assuming we've actually achieved any semblance of serenity in the first place. Why is it so hard to find peace in this world? Because we're looking *in this world.*

After his resurrection, before Jesus ascended into heaven, he left his disciples with something they'd never had before: peace. More specifically, he gave them *his* peace, a gift not of this world.

16

Whatever the world [...] be taken from us. Any security, ha[...] ary reprieve from suffering is just th[...] y the things of heaven are perma[...] be taken away.

Do not *let* your hea[...]ed, Jesus tells us. This means we have a ch[...] re the things with him that threaten your peace, a[...]en remember they have no hold on you. You are his, and his peace is yours. How can you choose peace in your situation today?

> Father, so many things threaten to
> take my peace every day. Thank
> you that your peace can be my
> peace when I choose it. I don't
> want my heart to be troubled,
> so help me give up the thoughts
> that are causing unrest. You give
> perfect peace when I focus my
> gaze on you.

The Lord your God
is living among you.
He is a mighty savior.
He will take delight
in you with gladness.
With his love,
he will calm
all your fears.
He will rejoice over you
with joyful songs.

Zephaniah 3:17 NLT

THE PATIENCE PIT

I waited and waited
and waited some more;
patiently, knowing God
would come through for me.
Then, at last, he bent down
and listened to my cry.

PSALM 40:11 TPT

We're not that good at waiting for anything these days. Yet, the reality is that waiting is a necessary part of life. We wait for people, we wait for events, and we wait for desires to be fulfilled. But do we recognize that waiting might also apply to our emotional lives? Do we hold on to hope that we can be rescued from a troubled heart?

King David described himself as being in a pit of miry clay, likely another of his despairing moments, perhaps even on reflection of his sins. He needed to be rescued, not necessarily from his enemies, but from his state of mind.

David says he *waited patiently,* understanding that he might not be instantly rescued. And he trusted that God alone would save him.

Do you feel as though your emotions are on slippery ground or that your thoughts are stuck in the miry clay? Are you willing to wait patiently for the great rescuer to lift you up and place your feet on solid ground? Take a moment today to ask God for his help, recognize the necessity of waiting, and trust him for the rescue.

> God, sometimes I feel like you so
> far away. But in your Word you
> tell me that you are always near;
> you never leave me. I believe that
> today. I ask for your help and say
> that I will wait patiently for it.
> You will not disappoint me.

CREATURES OF HABIT

Do not conform to the pattern of this world, but be transformed by the renewing of your mind. Then you will be able to test and approve what God's will is—his good, pleasing and perfect will.

ROMANS 12:2 NIV

Wake up. Make bed. Get dressed. Coffee. Not always in that order, but you can guarantee that many do those things every single morning. They might also bite their nails, anger easily, and stay up too late. Patterns are hard to break. We are, after all, creatures of habit, and unfortunately not all of those habits are good.

What do you do when you are confronted with a habit that is not positive? Do you recognize when you rely on something just because it makes you feel accepted, comforted, or in control? Sometimes we aren't even conscious of our habits until we try to give them up.

Scripture says that establishing the right pattern begins with the renewing of our minds. This means that we must first acknowledge the need for change, and then submit our way of thinking to resemble that of Christ.

What habits do you find yourself constantly trying to break? Can you trust God today to show you his good, pleasing, and perfect will as you submit your worldly patterns to him?

Father, I do have worldly patterns and habits that are hard to break. Help me to see your good, pleasing, and perfect will for my life and walk according to that each day.

MEDITATE ON GOODNESS

Whatever is true, whatever is honorable,
whatever is right, whatever is pure,
whatever is lovely, whatever is of good
repute, if there is any excellence
and if anything worthy of praise,
dwell on these things.

PHILIPPIANS 4:8 NASB

Do you ever catch yourself dwelling on the negative aspects of life? We can be nonchalant when someone tells us good news, but talk for hours about conflict, worries, and disappointment.

It is good to communicate things that aren't going so well in our lives, but we can also fall into the trap of setting our minds on the wrong things.

Paul saw the need to address this within the church of Philippi. It seems there were people in the church that thought too highly of themselves and allowed discord to reside in their midst. Think of what dwelling on the negative actually does: it creates feelings of hopelessness, discouragement, and a lack of trust in our God who is good, true, and just.

Can you find anything in your life and the lives of others that have virtue or are worthy of praise? Choose to dwell on the true, noble, just, pure, and lovely things, and experience the refreshing nature of a positive outlook.

**Father God, sometimes it's easier
to be negative than positive.
It's easy to look at everything
that is going wrong and forget
about all that is good. Today, help
me to shift my focus and start
seeing all of the excellence around
me. You have truly blessed me
with goodness.**

"Arise, my love,
my beautiful one,
and come away."

Song of Solomon 2:10 ESV

FULLY TRUSTING

Trust in the Lord with all your heart,
And lean not on your own
understanding;
In all your ways acknowledge Him,
And He shall direct your paths.

PROVERBS 3:5-6 NKJV

Trust can be a hard word to put into action mostly because our experience with others tells us that we can be sorely disappointed. People let us down in many ways. We can even be disappointed in ourselves.

Remember the trust game that involved standing with eyes closed and falling back into the hands of a few peers in hopes that they would catch you? There was risk involved in that game, and it didn't always turn out well.

Nothing can truly be guaranteed in this life, can it? Well, it depends on where you place your trust.

God watches over us, cares for us, and is involved in our lives. When we acknowledge that every good thing comes from him, our faith is strengthened and we are able to trust him more. Make a point of noticing how God directs your paths today, and thank him for being trustworthy.

Trust doesn't come easy, God. When I think about it, it seems crazy that I withhold trust from you—the one who created me and knows me intimately! I choose today to look at all the good places you have led me and continue to lead me. You are trustworthy and I thank you for that.

LOVE WITHOUT FEAR

*There is no fear in love. But perfect love
drives out fear, because fear has to do
with punishment. The one who fears is
not made perfect in love.*

1 John 4:18 NIV

God is an awesome God. He is all-powerful and he is
holy. When we compare ourselves to such greatness, we
can be overwhelmed with our insignificance. God is the
author of life and death, and he determines our eternity!

But we know that God is love, and because of his love,
he created a way for us to approach him boldly. He made
us righteous and holy through the redemption of Christ.

We are no longer in fear of punishment from a powerful
God. Human love can involve fear because it is not

perfect. It can disappoint, it can be taken away, and it can create a power imbalance that highlights our insecurities.

Do you compare God's love for you with the earthly love you have experienced? Acknowledge your struggle to accept God's perfect love. Allow yourself to love, and to be loved, without fear.

It can be a struggle to accept that you love me with a perfect love, Father. But I believe it because it says so in your Word, and your Word is truth. Help me to allow myself to be loved by you without fear of punishment.

PERFECT IN WEAKNESS

"My grace is sufficient for you, for power is perfected in weakness." Most gladly, therefore, I will rather boast about my weaknesses, so that the power of Christ may dwell in me.

2 CORINTHIANS 12:9 NASB

Have you ever taken a personality test to identify your strengths and weaknesses? You probably know if you are an introvert or extravert, whether you are creative or administrative, good at speaking, or great at listening.

You probably also know all too well what your weaknesses are. You might be over-analytical, self-doubting, unorganized, or lacking empathy. There are areas in our life that we certainly don't feel proud of!

Paul, on the other hand, says he would rather boast about his weaknesses! Paul knew that his weaknesses made him rely on the power of the Holy Spirit.

You may be facing something that you are worried about because it is outside of your comfort zone. It is not really the weakness in which you boast, but rather the power of Christ that is revealed through your weakness. Will you consider that God can shine through you as you acknowledge your complete reliance on his Holy Spirit?

God, I completely rely on your Holy Spirit to lead me through all areas of weakness. You can shine in and through me as I surrender my weaknesses wholly to you.

Faith comes from hearing, and hearing through the word of Christ.

Romans 10:17 ESV

COMPARISON

*Let everyone be sure that he is doing
his very best, for then he will have the
personal satisfaction of work well done
and won't need to compare himself
with someone else.*

GALATIANS 6:4 TLB

In the age of social media, comparison has become an easier default for us than it's ever been before. When every image we see of others has been properly angled, edited, filtered, and cropped we are quickly led into the delusion that the lives we see portrayed in those images are perfect.

We believe that the smiling faces we see in that post are always smiling, and the perfect homes with the beautiful lighting are permanently well-kept and polished.

The danger of these filtered images is that we end up comparing ourselves to something that isn't an accurate standard. What we don't see is the life outside that frame. We don't see the mess, the struggles, and the imperfections that are inevitably part of every life—even the perfect-looking ones.

God wants you to be so invested in the work that he has given you to do that you are not distracted or dissatisfied by what you see someone else doing. What does your unique lifestyle look like?

God, I dive headfirst into my uniqueness. I say yes to contentment and joy and move forward into greater fulfillment and happiness because you have chosen me to be just who I am. No more comparisons, God!

IMPOSSIBLE

Behold, I will do a new thing,
Now it shall spring forth;
Shall you not know it?
I will even make a road in the wilderness
And rivers in the desert.

ISAIAH 43:19 NKJV

What seems impossible to you today? What have you given up on, walked away from, and written off as absurd? What dreams have you let die simply because you felt they were unattainable?

Maybe our dreams, though they seem far off, were placed in our hearts for a purpose. And maybe they won't look exactly the way we always thought they would, but maybe they'll still come true in a new way.

Maybe the things that seem insurmountable to us will be easily overcome when we simply shift perspective and look at them differently.

Beloved, you serve a God who is powerful enough to make a path appear right through an empty wilderness and create a stream of life-giving water in the midst of a desert. He is more than able to take even the most impossible of situations and provide clarity, direction, and the means to make it through.

God, I trust you with my impossibilities and rely on your strength for my weaknesses.

FULLY ALIVE

*When you follow the revelation
of the Word,
heaven's bliss fills your soul.*

PROVERBS 29:18 TPT

Everyday living can suck the life right out of us.
Somewhere in the middle of being stuck in traffic,
sweeping floors, and brushing our teeth, we can forget
to be alive.

What does it mean to be *alive*, rather than just to live?
Not to only exist in life, but to know it, to understand
it, to experience it—to *live* it. What would it be like?
Freefalling from an airplane. Running through the grass
barefoot with sun on your face. Bringing babies into the
world, screaming and strong with power and life.

What would it be like if we lived each moment in the spirit of those fully alive moments?

Without a reason for life, without purpose, we perish. We falter. We lose our way. We lose hope. We begin to casually exist instead of breathing in the reverence of a fully alive life. What dreams has God given you that you've lost along the way?

> God, I trust that the dreams you gave me and I've somehow lost will be returned to me. You breathed life into me so that I could live to the fullest. I want that too.

Psalm 69:32 NLT

The humble will see their God at work and be glad. Let all who seek God's help be encouraged.

A WAY OUT

*No temptation has overtaken you except
what is common to mankind. And God
is faithful; he will not let you be tempted
beyond what you can bear. But when you
are tempted, he will also provide a way
out so that you can endure it.*

1 CORINTHIANS 10:13 NIV

Each of us struggles with temptation. No one is exempt.
From gossip to overindulging, to unkind thoughts, and
more, we battle with temptation in all different ways.

The good news is that we serve a God who is faithful,
and, oh, how he loves his children! The Bible tells us
that he won't allow us to be faced with more than what
we can handle. When we turn to him in the midst of our
struggles, we can find our way out.

Be prepared for your time of battle by praying for protection. Ask the Lord to open your eyes to see the ways in which you may fall, so that you can be ready to face them head on. Though temptation will surely come your way, be assured that it will not overcome you as you trust in the Lord.

God, when the way out of temptation doesn't seem clear, give me your eyes. I know I am blinded by the world in moments of struggle and I need you to reach down, grab my hand, and lead me to the emergency exit. I trust you to help me.

HE HEARS

This is the confidence we have in
approaching God: that if we ask anything
according to his will, he hears us.
And if we know that he hears us—
whatever we ask—we know that
we have what we asked of him.

1 JOHN 5:14-15 NIV

Sometimes it can feel as if God is far away: an elusive
man in the heavens who is so far above us that surely he
cannot be interested in our day-to-day lives. Our desires
and requests seem so small by comparison that it seems
unworthy a task to even ask him for help. But he is a
God who loves his children. He wants us to be happy, to
feel fulfilled.

The best way to know if something is true, or right, is to
hear it for yourself—straight from the source. You believe

you nailed the interview, but you don't believe you got the job until you get the phone call. The same is true for bad news, at least ideally. You get wind of a rumor about a friend's indiscretion, but you wait for her side of the story before believing a word.

So what about God? How can we hear from him? How do we discern his will for our lives? We may not have a hotline, but we do have his book. God speaks to us through his Word, so if you are waiting for confirmation, direction, validation, or conviction, pick it up.

Allow yourself to be filled with God's presence. He loves you and wants the best for you. What do you want from God today? If you ask in his will, he will answer you.

Father God, you really do hear me. You tell me I can have confidence approaching you when I ask for your will in my life because you listen. But you don't just listen. You also give. Your blessings are abundant and your grace is sufficient. Thank you.

REST SECURE

I keep my eyes always on the LORD.
With him at my right hand,
I will not be shaken.
Therefore my heart is glad
and my tongue rejoices;
my body also will rest secure.

PSALM 16:8-9 NIV

A loud crash in the night. Unexpected footsteps falling uncomfortably close in a dark parking lot. A ringing phone at 3:00 AM. No matter how brave we think we are, certain situations quicken the pulse. We've heard, over and over, that we have nothing to fear if we walk with God, but let's be honest: certain situations are scary! So what does it mean to rest secure in the Lord?

No matter where you are, God is there also. While there may be times when we ache to hide from him in our shame, he is a constant presence. The beautiful thing about his omnipresence is that we have a steady and consistent companion who is always ready to help in times of trouble.

We have no reason to fear the things that the world may throw our way. We've got the best protector of all at our side! Are you asking for his help in times of worry and woe, or are you turning inward to try to solve your problems?

Let God be your refuge. Nothing is too big or too small for him! Even in your darkest hours, you can know true joy because he is your guardian. Take your cares and distress, and cast them upon him today because he can handle it. Rest secure in him.

God, when I look to the world for comfort and encouragement, I come up empty. Nothing can fill me or protect me like you can. You are by my side and you make me glad. I rejoice in your goodness and peace today.

I am confident of this very thing, that He who began a good work in you will perfect it until the day of Christ Jesus.

Philippians 1:6 NASB

MELODY OF WORSHIP

God's splendor is a tale that is told;
his testament is written in the stars.
Space itself speaks his story every day
through the marvels of the heavens.
His truth is on tour in a starry-vault of the sky,
showing his skill in creation's craftsmanship.
Every day gushes out its message to the next,
night with night whispering its knowledge to all.
Without a sound, without a word,
without a voice being heard,
Yet all the world can see its story.
Everywhere its gospel is clearly read
so all may know.

PSALM 19:1-4 TPT

Have you ever felt the song of your heart praising the Lord? No words may come, no verses, no chorus, and yet your very being feels as though it may burst from the music inside you. You are not alone! Even the very heavens praise him in this way!

The Bible tells us that without words, and without even the slightest sound, the skies burst forth in a song of praise for the glory of God. Isn't that an amazing picture? Can't you just envision an orchestra above you?

Break forth into your song! Allow your heart to feel the words, even if you cannot fully form them. Give God all your praises today. He is so deserving of them! Let your heart be a celebration of your love for Jesus Christ. Give in to the melody of worship inside you.

Father, regardless of how my voice sounds to others, when I pour out my worship before you, you hear a beautiful melody—a masterpiece even! I sing my song of praise to you today because you are worthy of all praise.

UNFAILING GOODNESS

> "I am about to go the way of all the
> earth, and you know in your hearts and
> souls, all of you, that not one thing has
> failed of all the good things that the LORD
> your God promised concerning you; all
> have come to pass for you, not one of
> them has failed."
>
> JOSHUA 23:14 NRSV

Do you remember the first thing that you failed at?
Maybe it was a test at school, a diet, a job interview, or
even a relationship. Failure is difficult to admit, especially
in a culture that values outward success and appearance.

We often hear it said that success comes from many
failures, but we only really hear that from successful people!

When Joshua was advanced in years, he reminded the Israelites of all that God had done for them. Though they had been unfaithful to God many times, God remained faithful, and they became a great nation that none could withstand.

God had a plan and a purpose for the nation of Israel, and through his power and mercy he ensured that these plans succeeded. In the same way, God has a purpose for your life, and while you may fail, he will not.

> **God, I take the opportunity today
> to submit my heart to your will.
> Not one good thing that you have
> planned for me will fail. Not one.**

ETERNAL FOUNTAIN

*"Whoever drinks of the water that I shall
give him will never thirst. But the water
that I shall give him will become in him
a fountain of water springing up into
everlasting life."*

JOHN 4:14 NKJV

We take it for granted that when we turn on a faucet,
water will come out. If we need something to drink,
we can quench our thirst pretty easily. In Jesus' day,
however, people (usually women) had to get their water
from the well, often situated quite a walk away from their
homes. It was a necessary daily task that provided for the
family's needs.

Imagine then, being offered water that would last forever.
This is what Jesus offered the woman at the well. She

would never have to make this trip again in the heat of the day. She wanted this answer to her need. Jesus compared her desire with a spiritual desire: just as the well was a source for physical life, he was the source for eternal life.

You have received Jesus as the source for your life. Not only does Jesus say that he will provide you with everlasting water, but he says that this water will be like a fountain, springing up.

Father, I am so thankful for the eternal life that you have placed within me. I draw from you as my source of life today.

The Lord
is near to all
who call on him,
to all who call
on him
in truth.

Psalm 145:18 NIV

BUSYNESS

"Come away by yourselves to a secluded place and rest a while." (For there were many people coming and going, and they did not even have time to eat.)

MARK 6:31 NASB

We are all well acquainted with stress. There are so many things in our life that cause us to be worried, pressured, and anxious. The world constantly presents us with unknowns and predicaments that steal our joy and rob our peace. Our lives are so full that we often have difficulty finding time to spend with Jesus.

When we get in the presence of God and spend time in his Word, we are able to escape the stress of our lives and place our problems in his hands. God gives a peace that is unlike anything the world offers. He is focused on preparing us for his permanent kingdom, and, as a result, his presence offers hope and everlasting joy that is opposite to the trivial stressors of this life.

God, who has existed for eternity, is not bound by time. Because he is outside of time, time does not limit him the way that it limits us. When we take even a few sacred minutes to spend in his presence in the midst of our busy day, he can meet us there and download deep truths to our hearts.

Spend time in his presence today, letting his peace wash over your heart. Focus on his truth and his capability rather than your problems and incapacity. What is troubling you? God is able exchange it for peace that is beyond what you can imagine.

God, I know that even in my busyness there is always time for you. I can choose to make my relationship with you a priority or I can choose to be too busy. I want to make the right choice. I want to spend time with you listening with an open heart so you can speak to me.

LIVING WORD

*The word of God is living and active and
sharper than any two-edged sword, and
piercing as far as the division of soul
and spirit, of both joints and marrow,
and able to judge the thoughts and
intentions of the heart.*

HEBREWS 4:12 NASB

Have you ever noticed God speaking to you in themes?
We all go through different seasons in life, and God
speaks to our hearts accordingly. Some of us may be
going through a season of learning to wait, while another
is learning how to step out in faith.

The beautiful thing about God is that he is big enough
to speak to all of us—in our different places, with our
different hearts—at the same time, with the same words.

God's Word is alive and active. It can deliver truth to the heart of each unique person. Two people can get something completely different from the same passage of Scripture because of what God has been doing in each of their hearts separately. Through the body of Christ, we can come together and share what God is teaching us—multiplying our individual growth as we encourage one another.

Never doubt the power of what you hold in your hands when you read the Word of God. Your Creator knows you so intimately because he is the one who handcrafted your soul.

Thank you, Father, that you care
about me enough to speak directly
to my heart through your living
Word. I want to hear what you have
to say to me today.

Those who love your instructions have great peace and do not stumble.

Psalm 119:165 NLT

SAND CASTLES

*"Don't store up treasures here on earth
where they can erode away or may be
stolen. Store them in heaven where they
will never lose their value and are safe
from thieves. If your profits are in heaven,
your heart will be there too."*

MATTHEW 6:19-21 TLB

Have you ever been sitting on a beach and watched a little child work tirelessly on an elaborate sand castle? They spend hours perfecting their creation, thoughtfully forming each section, often stepping back to admire their work.

These little children are unaware of the patterns of ocean waves and don't realize that as the day passes, their masterpieces will eventually be swept away by the swelling tide. All that work, all that concentration, all that pride, gone as the water erases the shore.

What proverbial castles are we building in our lives that could, at any moment, be simply erased? We've got to buy into the bigger vision. We must know what can last and what won't. There are temporary kingdoms and a kingdom that will never pass away. We have to recognize which one we are contributing to.

If your work and your heart are invested in a heavenly vision, then what you have spent your life on will continue to matter for longer than you live. Where is your treasure today?

Father, I want to spend my time investing in the eternal souls of people, in the eternal vision of advancing your kingdom, and in the never-ending truth of the Gospel. In these things, I will find purpose and treasure that will never be lost.

THE SPICE RACK

We know that in everything God works
for the good of those who love him.
They are the people he called,
because that was his plan.

ROMANS 8:28 NCV

Anyone who does any amount of cooking has a spice rack—that one place where all seasonings are kept within easy reach of the stovetop. There are some spices that get used consistently: garlic, salt, and pepper. And there are other spices that may only be used once in a while: cardamom, tarragon, anise. While those lesser-used spices may collect dust in the back of our spice cupboards, we still rely on them to bring out just the right flavor in that one particular meal.

Life is a lot like a spice rack. We shelve our experiences like spices: some make so much sense—like salt and pepper—we pull from them often, clearly recognizing their usefulness. Other experiences are more subtle and undeclared; sometimes we go years never understanding why we had them.

Then, in one moment, our life recipe will call for a little saffron. And all at once, it will make so much sense. That experience we had—the one we thought we must've had by mistake—will be the only one that matters for that moment.

Is there a season in your life that you often wonder about? You might look at that time and only see failure or waste. When you can't make sense of why it happened, remember that God will work it *all* for his good because you love him.

God, I admit I do wonder sometimes about different seasons of my life that have been challenging or confusing. I wonder how you are going to make good come out of them. If I haven't seen it already, I trust your Word that says good indeed will come because I love you.

SUSTAINED

I lay down and slept;
I awoke, for the Lord sustains me.

PSALM 3:5 NASB

There is always something to worry about, isn't there? Whether health, finances, relationships, or details, there are many unknowns in life that can easily keep us worrying.

But what if we stopped worrying? What if we stopped questioning and decided instead to feel peace? What if we could trust completely that God would take care of us and our loved ones? God is our rock and he alone will sustain us.

The words in Psalm 3 can bring us comfort and peace when we are fearful. It speaks volumes about the grace of God: the protection and safety of his hand. But the verse goes beyond peace and comfort to the *power* of

God. We only wake up because of his sustaining power. When we trust and believe in this God who possesses the power of life and death, what do we have to fear? Our entire lives are in his hands. We can't change that fact, so we might as well rest in it.

There will be many unknowns in your life. There will be moments when the rug feels as though it's been pulled out from under you, and there is nothing to do but despair. In those moments that you can't control, you *can* trust. What are you worried about right now?

**God, I take my worry right now
and place it in your hands. I rest my
soul, my mind, and my body in you.
You alone have the power
to sustain me.**

With my
whole heart
I seek you;
let me not
wander
from your
commandments!

Psalm 119:10 ESV

STUMBLING IN THE DARK

*The Word gave life to everything
that was created,
and his life brought light to everyone.
The light shines in the darkness,
and the darkness can never extinguish it.*

JOHN 1:4-5 NLT

Have you ever walked somewhere in the pitch black? You bump into things, knock stuff over, and often can't even place where you are or where you're going. Everything becomes muddled in the darkness. Without light to guide us, we can't see where we're going, or what we're running into.

Many times throughout the Bible, God likens being in sin to being in darkness. When we immerse ourselves in sin, thus rejecting the light of the truth, we can no longer see what we are running into.

Darkness will cloud our thinking and our rationale, and we won't even be able to determine what sins are coming our way. By allowing sinful messages to enter our souls through different avenues, we lose our ability to navigate our lives.

When wickedness begins to overtake your life, you lose the ability to recognize what is making you sin. Strive to keep your soul sensitive to the truth. Keep sight of the light by spending time in God's Word.

Father, I don't want to stumble around in the dark. I don't need to. Your light is bright, and pure, and forever. Help me prioritize spending time with you so I can stay close to you in the light.

HEART CENTER

If then you have been raised with Christ,
seek the things that are above, where
Christ is, seated at the right hand of
God. Set your minds on things that are
above, not on things that are on earth.

COLOSSIANS 3:1-2 ESV

Social media: an escape, a gift, a communicative tool, a joy stealer, a comparison thief, a comedian, entertainment. Social media can be fun! But it can also become an idol when we don't recognize it as such.

Suddenly, instead of opening up our Bible, we are clicking on our phones checking Facebook, posting photos and status updates to seek attention and approval from people rather than our Creator.

God's desire for our life is that we chose him above all else. He wants to be our focal point, one we return to time and again, so we don't ever steer too far off course. Instead of seeking approval from others, let's turn our eyes toward the one who loves us most, whose voice is the only one we should hear.

Where do you choose to spend the majority of your time? What choices could you eliminate to stay centered on Jesus? In a busy life of choices, it's important to know your back-up is also your best option—seeking God and choosing life with him.

> **Although communicating with people is necessary and fun, what I need more is you, God. Before I seek approval from others, I want to share my heart with you and hear what you have to say.**

I have swept away your offenses like a cloud, your sins like the morning mist. Return to me, for I have redeemed you.

Isaiah 44:22 NIV

THE VOICE OF LOVE

"The Father gives me the people who
are mine. Every one of them will come to
me, and I will always accept them."

JOHN 6:37 NCV

When we live for other voices, we will quickly become worn out and discouraged. Other people's expectations for how we should live, act, and be are sometimes unreachable.

There is one voice that matters, and it can come in a variety of forms—the voice of God.

What God would tell us is that we are loved, we are cherished, and we have significant value. We are his beloved, his children, his beautiful creation. This is the voice that matters. This is the voice to come back to when we feel like we're not enough.

What are the voices you typically listen to? Can you ignore them and focus only on the voice that matters? He will encourage you and remind you that you are enough. Nothing you do or don't do is going to make him love you any more or any less. Soak it in, so you can drown out all the other voices.

Father, I want your voice to be the loudest voice in my head. I want to be guided by you. I know you love me just as I am. You say that I am enough because you have made me enough through the work of the cross. Thank you.

BREAK EVERY CHAIN

*"His purpose in all of this is that they
should seek after God, and perhaps feel
their way toward him and find him—
though he is not far from any one of us."*

ACTS 17:27 TLB

There is a chance to start over—every day if we need to. From the inside out, we can be transformed and our hearts renewed. We can essentially remake ourselves with the help, healing, and transformative nature of Christ! Jesus died on the cross to promise us a life free from the bondage of sin, free from hopelessness, free from any chains that try to trap us. In Christ, we are set free.

It can be hard to understand the complete grace offered at Calvary because we are incapable of giving that kind of grace. But when God says that he has forgotten our sin, and that he has made us new, he really means it. God is love, and love keeps no record of wrongs. Nothing can keep us from his love. Salvation tore the veil that separated us from the holiness of God. That complete work cannot be diminished or erased by anything we do.

We need to hear the truth of Christ's promise for us and stop the cycle of hopelessness, defeat, and bondage to sin. All we need to do is get on our knees and pray.

Is there an area of your life that you need to receive freedom from? Wait for God's voice to permeate the deepest, saddest parts of you. He wants you to let him take care of you. He is pursuing your heart.

God, I know that I can only find
freedom in you. Thank you for
loving me enough to set me free
and help me with every struggle.
Let me hear your voice speaking
to my heart today.

I have
redeemed you;
I have called you
by name,
you are mine.

Isaiah 43:1 ESV

GLORIOUS

On the glorious splendor
of your majesty,
and on your wondrous works,
I will meditate.

PSALM 145:5 NRSV

Leaves changing from green to orange to red. Gently falling snow. A rainbow-colored sunrise. A sprout of newness in the dirt. The smell of freshly cut grass. The rustling of leaves in the trees. The smell of a pine tree at Christmas time. Billowy, moving clouds. Sunshine kissing your cheeks. It is amazing that our Creator would make all of this for us to enjoy. It's glorious, really.

Yet, days can go by and we haven't stopped to notice. We forget to slow down. We ignore this incredibly beautiful world that he made for us to explore and enjoy.

It is amazing what a walk with a friend, a run through the woods, or the feel of bare feet on grass can do for our soul.

Do you take time to get outside and enjoy all that he created?

The next time you're feeling a bit squirmy, slow down, take a walk outside, and soak in his presence that's all around you: in the grass between your toes, in the rustle of leaves above you, and in the sunshine kissing your cheeks.

God, you have made everything so beautiful. Thank you for the joys in simple life—for the beauty in every tiny detail of your creation. When I take time to stop and ponder your works, I am awestruck. You are amazing.

GOD'S EAR

I love the LORD, for he heard my voice;
he heard my cry for mercy.
Because he turned his ear to me,
I will call on him as long as I live...
Then I called on the name of the LORD:
"LORD, save me!"
The LORD is gracious and righteous;
our God is full of compassion.
The LORD protects the unwary;
when I was brought low, he saved me.
Return to your rest, my soul,
for the LORD has been good to you.

PSALM 116:1-7 NIV

God hears you. Whether you are shouting praises of thanksgiving, crying tears of mourning, or singing phrases of glory, God hears. He listens. He does not abandon or ignore.

He hears your voice. He hears your heart. He hears your shouts, your whispers, and your thoughts. Sometimes this seems scary; we feel like we have to perform. That is a lie. Do not believe it. God takes us as we are, where we are. We don't have to filter, pretend, or please. He meets us, loves us, accepts us just as we are in this moment.

Do you believe God hears you? What do you want to tell him right now? He is a beautiful, caring God who takes us as sinners and holds our hand as we walk the path to salvation.

Father God, thank you for listening to me in all my different emotions. You are full of compassion and you have been so good to me. I am so blessed to be called your child.

Those who know
Your name
will put their trust
in You;
for You, Lord,
have not forsaken
those who
seek You.

Psalm 9:10 NKJV

REST IN JESUS

He who dwells in the secret place
of the Most High
Shall abide under the shadow
of the Almighty.

PSALM 91:1 NKJV

Have you ever been awake when you think no one else is? Maybe you had an early morning flight, and you feel you are the only person who could possibly be stirring at that hour. It feels kind of magical, doesn't it? It's like you have an unshared secret.

Regardless of you being a night owl, morning person, or somewhere in-between, there is peace that comes with meeting Jesus in secret—when your world has stopped for a bit.

Whatever it looks like, rising early or staying up late, taking a work break, a study break, or a mommy break, finding that quiet is where you can actually acquire strength. We need spiritual food to conquer each day.

Can you find daily quiet time to meet with Jesus? He will meet you in that space, filling you with peace, strength, and love to go out and conquer the world.

Meeting with you in my secret place is so refreshing, Lord. You fill my heart with hope and give me everything I need to get through each day. Thank you that I can find rest in you.

CHANGE OF SEASON

"Be strong and courageous, and act; do not fear nor be dismayed, for the Lord God, my God, is with you. He will not fail you nor forsake you until all the work for the service of the house of the Lord is finished."

1 Chronicles 28:20 NASB

The change of seasons can bring a variety of feelings. Hope, anxiety, excitement, expectation, or worry can knock at your door each time the weather changes. Just as the physical season shifts are natural and needed, spiritual and emotional seasons are necessary as well.

You will experience various seasons in your life: seasons of longing and contentment, seasons of discouragement and joy, seasons of more and less. Being a grown-up means stretching into new ways of living, and this usually doesn't happen until the season hits.

Seasons can be challenging. They require bravery, obedience, dedication, and sometimes total upheaval of everything comfortable in our lives. If we feel that impending corner of a season change in our hearts, it usually means God is preparing us for something different—a *change*. In those seasons of life, the one who won't change, won't back down, and won't leave us stranded is our heavenly Father.

Do you see an impending season change approaching? How does it make you feel? Be brave! God will not move you into something without giving you the grace you need to make it through.

Just like with natural seasons, God, there are some spiritual seasons I like better than others. Winter is hard. Spring is hopeful. But I know you have blessings and intentions for each season of life I'm in. Help me see your purposes and rejoice in them.

JOYOUS JOURNEY

*Consider it pure joy, my brothers and
sisters, whenever you face trials of many
kinds, because you know that the testing
of your faith produces perseverance.
Let perseverance finish its work so that
you may be mature and complete,
not lacking anything.*

JAMES 1:2-4 NIV

There is great joy in the journey: in the mundane details,
in the difficult times, in the confusing moments, and in
the tears. There is so much joy to be found in the quiet
and in the noise.

Pity parties and comparisons create a direct path for the
enemy to steal our joy. There is hope in Jesus and the gift
of little joy-filled moments. They come in varying forms:
sunshine rays pouring in the windows, a nice person at

the check-out counter, a turn-the-radio-as-high-as-it-can-go kind of song, a dance party in the living room, or the taste of a delicious meal after a long day.

Whatever the moment, there is joy if we look for it.

There's a journey of joy in waking up every day knowing it's another day to breathe in the fresh air, head to dinner with a girlfriend, or grab coffee with a co-worker. Find joy in the moment.

God, there really is joy to be found in every moment I am alive. You have blessed me with breath, friendship, and opportunity. Thank you for each new day and all the joy there is to be found in it.

The Lord bless you
and keep you;
the Lord make
His face shine on you,
and be gracious to you;
the Lord lift up
His countenance on you,
and give you peace.

Numbers 6:24-26
NASB

HE KNOWS WHEN WE DON'T

*The Spirit helps us with our weakness.
We do not know how to pray as we
should. But the Spirit himself speaks to
God for us, even begs God for us with
deep feelings that words cannot explain.*

ROMANS 8:26 NCV

You stare at the menu, overwhelmed by choices. Pasta sounds yummy, but you're avoiding gluten. Salad sounds healthy, but you just had that for lunch. Steak sounds perfect until you look at the price. Everyone else has ordered; all eyes are on you. You know you're hungry, just not what *for*.

"What do I want?" you ask, though not expecting an answer.

106

There are days prayer can feel like that. We know we want something—we sense an ache or longing—but can't quite identify it. Other times, we're simply in too much pain to focus. We need, we need... but we can't get the words out.

"What do I want?" we cry. This time, we *can* expect an answer. The Holy Spirit, because he lives inside us, knows us so intimately he can actually step in and pray on our behalf. He knows, even when we don't.

Spend some time with the Spirit today. Thank him for knowing your heart, and sharing it with God when you can't.

> God, I don't always have words
> for what is going on in my heart. I
> can come up with plenty of catch
> phrases and clichés, but those are
> meaningless at times. Thank you
> that you hear my heart and you
> speak for me. Do that for me today
> as I spend time with you.

BEING KNOWN

You know what I long for, LORD;
you hear my every sigh.

PSALM 38:9 NLT

Think of the most perfect gift you've ever received.
Not the most extravagant, but the one that was just so
perfectly *you* that you realized the giver really knew you.

Your gift giver heard you, that one time, when you
mentioned that one thing, perhaps in passing. And
because they were listening with their heart, they saw
into yours. They got you.

We love to be understood, and long to be seen. For
many of us it's how we know we are loved. How much,
then, must the Father love us? He who knows everything
about us—who takes the time to listen to every longing

and comfort every sigh—is waiting to give us his perfect gifts. We are known. We are loved.

Share your longing with God today. Let him show you his great love by revealing how intimately he knows you. Let him give you a good and perfect gift.

I'll admit, God, some days there are a lot of sighs coming from me. Thank you that you know what each sigh means, and you know exactly what I need. Your gifts are good and perfect because you know me better than anyone else and you love me fully.

We know
the love
that God
has for us,
and we trust
that love.

1 John 4:16 NCV

IN TIMES OF DOUBT

God you are near me always, so close to me;
every one of your commands reveals truth.
I've known all along how true and unchanging
is every word you speak, established forever!

Psalm 119:151-152 TPT

The sun will set tonight; it will rise tomorrow. This is truth. We have no reason to doubt what we've witnessed every day of our lives. But when experience tells us otherwise, or perhaps we have no experience to go on, doubts creep in. It's going to snow tomorrow. "I doubt that," we say.

When someone we trust says they'll be there for us, we have faith in their words. Someone who has repeatedly let us down can make the same promise, but we remain uncertain until they've shown up and proven themselves. We're unsettled. We doubt. God wants to erase our doubt and he will; we only need to have faith.

God has given us a huge gift in his faithful nature. He promises us things and sticks to those promises without fail. It may feel easier to trust God in the big moments, the desperate moments. But in everyday moments, we can also press into him without restraint. He will carry us as he promises.

How beautiful is this God! His every command reveals truth. Examine your prayer life. Do you trust God, or do you doubt his promises to you? Why? Share your heart openly with him, and ask him for unwavering faith.

God, I need faith that doesn't waver. Sometimes it's hard to see that you are fulfilling your promises. Sometimes I doubt your goodness. And although those feelings are real, they are not true. You will fulfill everything you have promised, and you are always good. I choose to believe those truths today.

PLEASE REMAIN SEATED

"Remain in me, as I also remain in you.
No branch can bear fruit by itself; it must
remain in the vine. Neither can you bear
fruit unless you remain in me."

JOHN 15:4 NIV

When riding in a moving car, boat, or plane, we wouldn't just jump out, no matter how restless or impatient we were feeling. That would be crazy. We couldn't possibly expect to arrive at our destination as safely or as quickly— or perhaps at all. We grasp the necessity of remaining where we are if we are to get where we are going.

Why, then, are we so quick to jump ahead when it comes to God's plans for our lives? We accept his grace, but not his timing. We welcome his comfort, but not his discipline.

How often do we decide without praying, or act without his prompting? And yet we expect to get where we are going—safely, quickly, easily.

Are there areas of your life you are trying to direct on your own? Spend some time praying for the Spirit to reveal to you anywhere you are not abiding in Jesus, or trusting his timing. Ask him to help you trust him.

God, I confess my need to control my schedule and my life. I want to give this over to you and let you show me where I could abide in you better. I trust you to do what is perfect for me, and that means I have to trust your timing. Help me in this, Lord.

TRUST THE LIGHT

"I am the Light of the world; he who follows Me will not walk in the darkness, but will have the Light of life."

JOHN 8:12 NASB

Imagine yourself in total darkness, perhaps a wilderness camping trip (or a power failure at a nice hotel if that's more your speed). It's the middle of the night, and you must find your way back to camp.

Turn on your flashlight. Though it only illuminates a few steps at a time, it's enough to keep moving. Each step forward lights more of the way, and eventually, you see your destination.

Our faith walk is very much like this. Most of the time, we can't see where we're headed. Although just a few steps ahead is all we can make out for certain, we trust the path the light reveals.

Jesus is our light. He shows us just what we need to see to put one foot forward at a time. Ask him to help you ignore the unseen and trust the light.

God, just as I see better in the darkness with a flashlight to illuminate my path, I see better when I let you shine on my life and show me the best way to proceed. When it's hard to put one foot in front of the other, give me the grace and strength to continue.

OUR COMFORTER

*Praise be to the God and Father of
our Lord Jesus Christ, the Father of
compassion and the God of all comfort,
who comforts us in all our troubles,
so that we can comfort those in
any trouble with the comfort we
ourselves receive from God.*

2 CORINTHIANS 1:3-4 NIV

It's the end of a long, difficult day. All you want to do is crawl in bed, wrap up in your comforter, and rest. Something about a soft, fluffy blanket helps problems seem less like problems.

One of God's many names is the *God of all comfort*. He is our ultimate comforter, allowing us to wrap ourselves in him and be warmed, reassured, and relieved. He does this so we can pay it forward, wrapping ourselves around others in need of comfort, and showing them his love.

Notice the repetition in the verses above. The word *comfort* appears four times. This isn't because Paul was feeling uninspired; it's because he wanted to make sure we heard him. We are comforted so that we can comfort. God wants both for us. Which have you done more of lately? Ask him to help you with the other.

> **Whether being comforted,**
> **or comforting others, God,**
> **I need your compassion.**
> **That fills me with peace for myself**
> **and peace to pour out on others.**
> **Thank you that difficult situations**
> **are never wasted. You give me**
> **opportunities to share with others**
> **in their need for comfort.**

Even before
he made the world,
God loved us
and chose us
in Christ
to be holy
and without fault
in his eyes.

Ephesians
1:4 NLT

FINDING PEACE

*You will keep in perfect peace
all who trust in you,
all whose thoughts are fixed on you!*

ISAIAH 26:3 NLT

What does chaos look like in your world? Crazy work deadlines, over-scheduled activities, long to-do lists and short hours? All of the above? How about peace? What does that look like?

Most of us immediately picture having gotten away, whether to the master bathroom tub or a sunny beach. It's quiet. Serene. The trouble with that image, lovely as it is, is that it's fleeting.

We can't live in our bathtubs or in Fiji, so our best bet is to seek out peace right in the middle of our chaos. Guess what? We can have it. Jesus promises peace to all who put him first.

How appealing is it to imagine being unmoved by the stresses in your life? Is it easy or difficult for you to claim this promise for yourself? Ask Jesus to grant you true peace; fix your thoughts on him and watch the rest of the world fade away. When it tries to sneak back in, ask him again.

God, finding true peace in this crazy world is impossible. I can relax in the hot sun and warm water on a tropical island for a week, but the peace found there is still only temporary. Lasting peace only comes from keeping my mind fixed on you. That's the peace I want.

WHERE CREDIT IS DUE

"Give praise to the LORD,
proclaim his name;
make known among the nations
what he has done,
and proclaim that his name
is exalted.
Sing to the LORD,
for he has done glorious things;
let this be known to all the world."

ISAIAH 12:4-5 NIV

You achieve a goal, or you get some wonderful news. The day you've been waiting for has arrived, and you're so excited about it. What is your first reaction? Do you update your status on social media to let your friends know what you've done? Do you call up your mom and tell her the wonderful news?

There's nothing wrong with sharing your excitement with others. But when doing so, be sure to first give the glory and praise to God. He has given you everything you have. Get excited about how good he has been to you.

When you're just so happy that you can't help but dance for joy, be sure to give Jesus a twirl too. He wants to celebrate with you!

Are you giving credit where it's due? Be sure to take some time today to thank the Lord for all that he has helped you achieve and for all that he has given you. He wants to share in your excitement!

Thank you, God, for everything that you have helped me to accomplish. You have done many great things in and through my life and you deserve all the glory for them.

WEARY TO THE CORE

The steps of the God-pursuing ones
follow firmly in the footsteps of the Lord.
And God delights in every step
they take to follow him.
If they stumble badly they will still survive,
for the Lord lifts them up with his hands.

PSALM 37:23-24 TPT

Have you ever been run so ragged that you just didn't know if you could take even one more step? Your calendar is a blur of scheduled activities, your days are full, your every hour is blocked off for this or that, and it's hard to find even a spare minute for yourself. Even your very bones feel weary, and you fall into your bed at night, drained from it all.

There is someone who is ready to catch you when you fall. You might stumble throughout your busy day, but he will never let you hit the floor as you take a tumble.

God delights in you! He will direct your every step if you ask him to. He will gladly take you by the hand and guide you.

Are you allowing the Lord to guide your days? Though you may be weary, he has enough energy to get you through it all. Hold out your hand to him today and walk side-by-side with Jesus.

Never-ending energy sounds
incredible, God. And you have it!
Help me to draw from you each
day so I have the energy needed to
live my life in a way that brings you
honor and glory. You can sustain
me in my weakest moments.

LOSING TO GAIN

*"If you try to hang on to your life, you
will lose it. But if you give up your life for
my sake, you will save it."*

MATTHEW 16:25 NLT

The key to growing in your faith is simple. There must be less of *us* in order to have more of God. To allow more of his presence into our lives, we must give up more of ourselves. We need to place our lives before him as an offering and give him our all.

The world would say that giving up ourselves is a loss. We've been taught for years that we must put ourselves first. Our fellow man would say that we need to make ourselves a priority. But oh, are they missing out!

When we give ourselves over completely to God, we get to share in his glory and in his great joy. Setting aside our earthly pleasures for heavenly treasures means we gain a lot more than what this world could ever offer us.

What desires do you find yourself holding onto? Empty yourself of the desires of your flesh and allow God to fill you with his presence. You won't feel a lack. In fact, it will overflow in your life, spilling out everywhere for others to see!

God, losing my life sounds scary. All around me, the world says I should make decisions that benefit me, that I should do everything I can to better my position in life. The reality is that I can only truly find my life by giving it to you. Help me to keep this perspective at the front of my mind.

The Lord
is good to all,
and his mercy
is over
all that he
has made.

Psalm 145:9 ESV

IN SUNSHINE
AND STORM

When times are good, be happy;
but when times are bad, consider this:
God has made the one
as well as the other.
Therefore, no one can discover
anything about their future.

ECCLESIASTES 7:14 NIV

It's easy to feel happy on a sunny day, when all is well, the birds are singing, and life is going along swimmingly. But what happens when waters are rougher, bad news comes, or the days feel just plain hard?

God wants us to feel gladness when times are good. He has made each and every day. We are called to rejoice in all of them whether good or bad. Happiness is determined by our circumstances, but true joy comes when we can find the silver linings, hidden in our darkest hours—when we can sing his praises no matter what.

We don't know what the future holds for us here on earth, but we can find our delight in the knowledge that our eternity is set in beauty.

Is your happiness determined by your circumstance?

God, help me discover true joy in
you, my Creator. Give me a deep and
abiding satisfaction in each day that
goes beyond human understanding.
I don't want my joy to be dependent
on my circumstances. My joy is
found in you.

WE HAVE TIME

Be careful how you live. Don't live like fools, but like those who are wise. Make the most of every opportunity in these evil days. Don't act thoughtlessly, but understand what the Lord wants you to do.

EPHESIANS 5:15-17 NLT

Time is one of those things we never seem to have enough of. Many of our days can feel like a race against the clock to get everything done. We seem to lack the time we need for even the most important things—things like being in God's Word, spending intentional time with loved ones, or volunteering to help those in need.

At the end of the day, there is one reality we must remember: we have time for what we make time for.

It's easy to feel busy, but what are we truly busying ourselves with? Are we finding time to spend browsing social media or watching re-runs of our favorite TV shows? Are we finding time to take a long shower or sleep for a few extra minutes in the morning? None of those things are necessarily *wrong*, but if we feel pressed for time and are unable to spend time with the Lord, we may need to rethink where our time goes.

Take a good hard look at your day today. How can you spend your time wisely—in a way that will make the most of the moments and opportunities you have.

God, help me to be wise with my choices today. I want to make the most of the opportunities you have put before me. I don't want to waste time or resources on things that do not matter. Show me where to put my efforts so they are blessed.

A THANKFUL HEART

Whatever you do, whether in word or deed, do it all in the name of the Lord Jesus, giving thanks to God the Father through him.

COLOSSIANS 3:17 NIV

Have you ever noticed on vacation that your heart feels lighter? That you worry less and are more thankful? Cultivating a heart of thankfulness can shift our entire perspective on life.

When we are grateful, we start to see the light of God so much more. We start to see him *everywhere*.

A thankful heart is a heart that refuses to let the enemy in and deceive us. Suddenly, our circumstances seem not so terrible, our problems not so huge. A heart of gratitude glorifies God and keeps us centered on him. Just like on vacation, you can have that same perspective every day—even in the most mundane circumstances.

What can you do to start cultivating a heart of gratitude? A heart of thankfulness keeps you grounded in Christ, in communion with him, and allows you to live the fullest life he's designed for you.

> **I am thankful for all of the blessings you have placed in my life, God. You have surrounded me with goodness; I see that better when I have a heart of thankfulness. Let that be my default—gratitude!**

The Lord is my strength and my shield; my heart trusts in Him, and I am helped.

Psalm 28:7 NASB

VULNERABILITY

He gives us more grace.
That is why Scripture says:
"God opposes the proud
but shows favor to the humble."

JAMES 4:6 NIV

Some of the most substantial and ultimately wonderful changes in our lives come from moments of vulnerability: laying our cards on the table, so to speak, and letting someone else know how much they really mean to us.

But vulnerability takes one key ingredient: humility. And humility is not an easy pill to swallow.

Isn't it sometimes easier for us to pretend that conflict never happened than to face the fact that we made a mistake and wronged another person? It's not always easy to humble ourselves and fight for the resolution in an argument—especially when it means admitting our failures.

Who are you in the face of conflict? Do you avoid apologizing in an attempt to save face? Does your pride get in the way of vulnerability, or are you willing and ready to humble yourself for restoration in your relationships?

> God, you say that you will give
> favor and wisdom to the humble.
> Today, I humble myself for
> the sake of a restored relationship.
> Show me what that looks like
> and help me walk it out.

RIVER OF PEACE

"I am the LORD your God,
who teaches you what is best for you,
who directs you in the way you should go
...your peace would have been like a river,
your well-being like the waves of the sea."

ISAIAH 48:17-18 NIV

Where do you usually go to find peace? Is there a certain place? A certain person?

One of the greatest gifts of God is his undeniable, unfathomable peace. It is a deep well that comes with knowing and experiencing Jesus' love. No matter where we are, where we are going, and whatever we might be experiencing, his peace is greater.

Grasp how deep his well runs. Lasting peace and joy does not come in the world or people around you.

148

Although those can be comforting, true, transforming, and powerful peace can only come from our Father. And oh, how he loves when we come to his well.

Where do you usually turn for peace? Have you experienced the indescribable peace of God?

> When I walk in your way, Father, you
> lead me into what is best for me. You
> know that better than I do. Help me
> to understand the benefit of living in
> your will and surrendering my own.
> You are my peace.

THIRST FOR PURE WATER

I want more than anything
to be in the courtyards of
the LORD's Temple.
My whole being wants
to be with the living God.

PSALM 84:2 NCV

Have you ever noticed that the more consistently you drink water, the more your body thirsts for it? And the less you drink water, the less you consciously desire it. Though you still need water to live, you become satisfied with small amounts of it disguised in other foods and drinks.

For a body that has become accustomed to pure water on a daily basis, only straight water will quench its thirst.

The same principle applies to God's presence in our lives. The more we enter his presence, the more we long to stay there. The more we sit at his feet and listen to what he has to say, the more we need his Word to continue living. But if we allow ourselves to become satisfied with candy-coated truth and second hand revelation, we will slowly begin to lose our hunger for the pure, untainted presence of the living God.

Does your entire being long to be with God? Press into Jesus until you can no longer be satisfied with anything less than the purest form of his presence. Cultivate your hunger and your fascination with him until you crave him.

God, I want to spend my life feasting on your truth, knowing your character, and adoring your heart. Help me desire you—the purest form of water.

No eye has seen,
no ear has heard,
no mind has
imagined
what God has
prepared for those
who love him.

1 Corinthians 2:9 NLT

NO CONDEMNATION

Straightening up, Jesus said to her,
"Woman, where are they?
Did no one condemn you?" She said,
"No one, Lord." And Jesus said,
"I do not condemn you either. Go.
From now on sin no more."

JOHN 8:10-11 NASB

Most of us know the story of the woman caught in adultery. One of the intriguing moments was when Jesus was questioned about whether or not the adulteress should be stoned. Jesus' response was to stoop down and start writing in the dirt.

Though we don't know exactly what Jesus wrote that day, the action of stooping down defined one interpretation of the word *grace.*

As everyone else stood casting judgement, Jesus removed himself from the accusers, stooping low and occupying himself elsewhere. It spoke volumes about his lack of participation in the crowd's judgement.

Because of Jesus' distraction, the eyes of the onlookers were drawn off the woman, perhaps lifting a portion of her shame. With their attention focused on Jesus, he said the words that saved the woman's life: "Let him who has never sinned cast the first stone." One by one, the accusers walked away. Jesus was the only one qualified to throw a stone; he chose grace instead. And he does the same for you.

God, you are merciful and forgiving. Thank you that you lift my sin and shame and offer me forgiveness and hope. You do not condemn me or remind me of my sin. You forgive completely and draw me closer. I am so grateful to be called your child.

GROWTH

I do not mean that I am already as
God wants me to be. I have not yet
reached that goal, but I continue trying
to reach it and to make it mine.
Christ wants me to do that, which is
the reason he made me his.

PHILIPPIANS 3:12 NCV

Do you remember when you realized you had stopped growing? Your height was going to be your height, your shoe size your shoe size. This second fact was pretty thrilling for many of us; no more hearing Mom say, "That's too much to spend on shoes you'll outgrow in a few months." And so the collection began.

Not too long after our bones finish growing, we realize

the real growth is just getting started. As we become young women, friendships either deepen or fade away as we begin to figure out who we are.

No matter what your age is today, you are likely still working on different areas in your life. When you are growing in Christ, it's a process that never really ends. You don't wake up one day and say, "I have arrived." The older you get, the more you realize how much you have to learn and grow.

How does knowing that God wants to help you become your best inspire you to attempt it?

Father God, help me as I continue
to grow in all different areas of
my life. Give me a teachable spirit
that causes a desire to be my very
best. I want to grow under your
guidance and care.

For the Lord God
is our sun
and our shield.
He gives grace
and glory.
The Lord will withhold
no good thing
from those who do
what is right.

Psalm 84:11 NLT